Railway Remnants

The Elham Valley Line

Peter Guise

Julie & Sue

Thank you for your support, encouragement, patience and understanding

(not to mention the raised eyebrows and occasional bouts of giggling!)

(oh yes! We did hear you!)

coming soon in this series

Railway Remnants

The East Kent Light Railway and The Crab & Winkle Line

(a double header)

Index

Photography Listing	6, 7, 8
Introduction	9
The Elham Valley Line: A brief history	10
Overview of the Line	10
From Canterbury West to South Canterbury	11
From South Canterbury to Bridge	19
From Bridge to Bishopsbourne	21
From Bishopsbourne to Barham	32
From Barham to Elham	35
From Elham to Lyminge	38
From Lyminge to Folkestone West	42
Peene Railway Museum	50
Bibliography	53
Acknowledgements	54

Photography Listing

Front Cover   Bishopsbourne Station

(the photo numbers also appear on the relevant OS map extract in their location)

Page	Photo	Photo Description
12	1	Canterbury West Station
12	2	Canterbury West Signal Box
13	3	Harbledown Junction
14	4	Across the Great Stour flood plain
14	5	The Great Stour Way
15	6	Toward Wincheap
15	7	Stour Bridge Abutment
15	8	Hambrook Marshes Sign
16	9 & 10	On Wincheap Industrial Estate
17	11	Wincheap Embankment
17	12	Site of Cow Lane Bridge
18	13	Wincheap (from Stupington Lane)
18	14	Stuppington Lane Bridge
18	15	Nackington Road Abutment
20	16	Bridge Road Abutments
20	17	Pett Bottom Road Bridge
20	18	Looking back toward the site of Bridge Station
22	19	Spire in the distance from the footpath
22	20	Bourne Tunnel - northern portal
23	21	Bishopsbourne Platform sign
24	22	Bishopsbourne Station from Crows Camp Bridge
24	23	Bishopsbourne Station Approach
25	24	Bishopsbourne Station - Entrance

Photography Listing

(the photo numbers also appear on the relevant OS map extract in their location)

Page	Photo	Photo Description
25	25	Bishopsbourne Station - Onto the down platform
26	26	Day trip to Canterbury?
26	27	Bishopsbourne Station - Down platform
27	28	Bishopsbourne Station - platform furniture
27	29 & 30	Bishopsbourne Station - posters
28	31	Bishopsbourne Station - looking toward Canterbury
28	32	Bishopsbourne Station - looking toward Folkestone
29	33	Bishopsbourne Station - weighing apparatus
29	34	Bishopsbourne Station - Up platform
30	35	Bishopsbourne Station - booking offices now kitchen
30	36	Bishopsbourne Station - offices now buffet
31	37	Bishopsbourne Station - To The Trains!
31	38	Bishopsbourne Station - Down platform signal—train due?
33	39	Covet Lane Bridge
33	40	Footpath alongside embankment
33	41	Footpath toward Barham
34	42	Barham - Railway Hill
34	43	Barham - Station site bridge remains
34	44	Barham Signal Box (now at the EKLR)
36	45	The Elham Valley route
36	46	Wingmore / Bladbean bridge
36	47	Site of the 'Worlds Wonder Bridge'
37	48	Approaching Elham
37	49	At Elham

Photography Listing

(the photo numbers also appear on the relevant OS map extract in their location)

Page	Photo	Photo Description
37	50	Looking down on the former Elham Station site
39	51	Ottinge Bridge (EVL 2081)
39	52	Ottinge Bridge (EVL 2081) from adjacent Elham Valley Way
40	53	Ottinge Bridge (EVL 2082)
40	54	Ottinge Bridge (EVL 2082) view over parapet looking south
41	55	Lyminge Station
41	56	Lyminge Station with part up platform
43	57	Greenbanks Bridge
43	58	Trackbed dumping ground
44	59	Peene Railway Museum
45	60	Etchinghill Tunnel - Southern Portal
46	61	Trackbed walking path between Peene & Etchinghill
46	62	Trackside drainage inspection pit
47	63	Peene Bridge
48	64	Channel Tunnel Rail Link Terminal
48	65	Cheriton Halt (site of)
49	66	Folkestone West (formerly Shorncliffe)
50	67	Peene Railway Museum
50	68	Peene Countryside Centre
50	69	Inside the Peene Countryside Centre
51	70	Elham Station Sign (Running In Board)
51	71	Bishopsbourne Station Sign (Running In Board)
51	72	Model of Lyminge Station
51	73	Model of Elham Station
51	74	Model of 'Worlds Wonder' Bridge
52	75-79	Model of English Terminal, Channel Tunnel Rail Link

Introduction

This is the first in a series of publications exploring the remnants of railways long past. It is not the intention of this series of guides to detail the history of these long forgotten dismantled railway lines. Nor is it intended to encourage the reader to discover routes for "walking the line," although it may be of benefit as a companion to those who are so inclined. In any event, there are a plethora of books on railway history and walks. Rather, it is hoped that what remains of railway lines once throbbing under the wheels of majestic locomotives will be documented and preserved, at least within these pages, before they are lost forever.

It may, nevertheless, provide a brief glimpse into the past of a dismantled railway and what remains of it today. Perhaps, it may encourage the reader to go see for oneself. The research and production of this guide has certainly satisfied my personal curiosity for a subject my grandfather was fond of talking about when I was a young lad in the early 1960s. It also got me out into the fresh air, well, for a while at least! It may also satisfy your curiosity and, maybe, explain the odd brick wall seen at the end of the road that appears to have no purpose at all or why a line of trees seems to have been planted between one street and another.

I recall my forebears, and others since, discussing the closure of railways, largely due to the Beeching Report, although it has to be pointed out that some lines were being closed, or being scheduled for closure, long before Dr. Beeching appeared on the platform.

The Elham Valley Line

A Brief History

The Elham Valley Railway ran from Canterbury to Folkestone and was so called as it ran through the Elham Valley. It connected the Ashford / Ramsgate mainline (at Harbledown, south west of Canterbury) with the Ashford / Folkestone mainline (at Cheriton, north west of Folkestone West.) This latter station name is its modern name having previously (and in the days of the Elham Valley Railway) been known as Shorncliffe. To add to the confusion, the modern Folkestone West is slightly further east than the old Shorncliffe (reputedly about 150 yards) and there was even a halt, called Cheriton Halt, some way short of the junction between the Elham Valley Railway and the mainline, east of the bridge that carries the Cheriton / Shorncliffe road. This halt was only ever used, however, by Elham Valley Railway trains! The section between Cheriton and Barham opened in July 1897 with the more difficult to construct Barham to Canterbury section opening two years later in July 1891. Services were finally withdrawn in June 1947 (pre Beeching!) and the line closed, having been reduced to single track sixteen years earlier. Like most railways of this nature it had also seen military service in both world wars. In the First World War it was used for troop movements to the channel port at Folkestone and in WWII it was home to a piece of big artillery known as the "Boche Buster."

Overview of the Line

I shall describe the route of the line from Canterbury to Folkestone although it was both constructed and opened in phases in the opposite direction; and closed in that direction for that matter. In fairness, however, it has to be pointed out that large sections of the route at either "end" have been obliterated by modern development of one kind or another. At the Canterbury end the line has given way to housing development and the Wincheap Industrial Estate whereas at the Folkestone end the Channel Tunnel Rail Link complex, for drive on drive off facilities, has completely taken over. It is at this end of the line, however, that the excellent Elham Valley Line Trust has its headquarters at Peene, open to the public for part of the year for the viewing of memorabilia and all things related to the Elham Valley Railway. It is interesting that the standard journey time between Canterbury West and Folkestone Central on the Elham Valley Line was about 50 minutes, a quarter of an hour faster than the replacement bus service; the No. 17 between Canterbury and Folkestone Bus Stations, although the bus goes through the villages whereas some of the railway stations were a hike from the village centre.

From
Canterbury West
To
South Canterbury

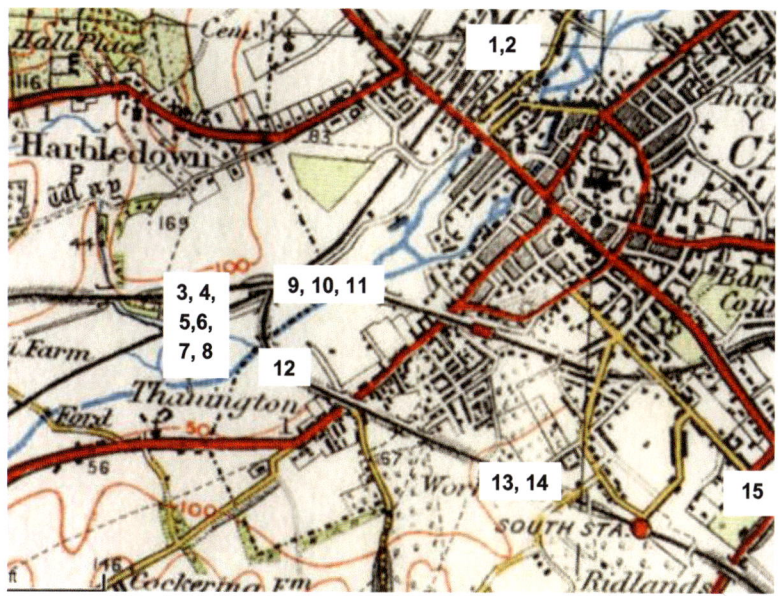

Reproduced from out of copyright OS Map 117 East Kent published 1938.

The northern terminus for the Elham Valley Line, Canterbury West, is on the mainline from Ashford (Ashford International) to Ramsgate. The station is now also served by hi-speed Javelin trains to St. Pancras International that have cut journey times to the capital to
less than an hour. This station was previously known as Canterbury. It received the "West" suffix following the opening of the line between Faversham and Dover that also had a Canterbury station, tagged as "East" to avoid obvious confusion.

Canterbury West also boasts this remarkable over the main line signal box; probably one of the few remaining on the national network. It is photographed here soon after restoration in the summer of 2012. Also seen in shot is the stabled stock for the Cathedrals Express excursion awaiting the return of its passengers and steam locomotive to haul it on the return trip to London Victoria.

The Elham Valley Railway left the Ashford to Ramsgate mainline at Harbledown Junction, just at the point where the Faversham to Dover line crossed over. The rails have long been lifted, of course, but the position of the points can be determined where the gaps in the third rail currently are, although, this is completely co-incidental as there were no third rails when the line closed! This view can be seen from beside a user operated crossing on Whitehall Way looking back toward Canterbury West.

The Elham Valley Line, from this point departed the mainline this side of the overbridge and bore to the viewer's right past the junction's signal box on its way to Wincheap. The signal box at the junction has long been dismantled and removed.

Leaving Harbledown Junction, the Elham Valley Railway curved out over the flood plain of the Great Stour toward Wincheap and the south of Canterbury on a vast embankment. Note the viaduct carrying the Faversham - Canterbury East - Dover line over the Hambrook Marshes in the right of the picture.

Now heavily overgrown, the embankment has been cut through to create a walking route to Chartham, not surprisingly called the Great Stour Way.

The old bridge over the River Stour has, of course, been demolished and removed but in this photograph, warehouse roofs on the vast Wincheap Industrial Estate can just be made out in the distance to the far right of the shot.

One bridge abutment remains on the bank of the Stour with a footpath forming part of the Great Stour Way.

At the base of the steps leading up to the embankment at this point is an information board that includes a photograph showing how substantial the bridge over the Great Stour was. It is mentioned here for reader reference as it is not the intention of this book to provide a complete (or even sketchy) 'before and after' record.

The Kent Enterprise Trust look after this site and each year the Hambrook Marshes Festival is held with stalls manned by local businesses, community and Arts & Crafts groups.

The Festival is usually held in July.

Now the line arcs round toward the Wincheap Industrial Estate, flirting with its southern edge. The obliteration of the line to the left of this photograph is all too clear but the old embankment can be seen to the right.

The second shot here shows the trackbed as it continues on toward the A28 Wincheap Road. When in use, there would have been no road and no bridge needed over it. In fact, the embankment has been removed to make way for the industrial use and the road.

Almost immediately, the trackbed has been built on at its approach to what would have been an enormous bridge to take the line over the busy Wincheap Road, the main A28 artery between Canterbury and Ashford. Indeed, this stretch of road is a regular contributor to the traffic updates on local radio warning road users of hold ups and congestion in the area. The Council's Social Services building on top of the embankment, in this reverse-angle shot, has also fallen into disrepair.

With the embankment and trackbed now at our backs we can view the site of the bridge across the Wincheap Road at its junction with Cow Lane and Hollow Lane. Much of the area has been flattened. Nevertheless, the straight line of trees, although interrupted where the bridge span would have been and where the new semi-detached houses have been built, rather gives the route away!

Redevelopment has included a community hall and car park and, on the other side of the main road, further housing has been built. The course of the Elham Valley Line is only visible in glimpses from this point on through the residential areas of Wincheap and Nunnery Fields although it does run almost parallel to the rear of gardens in Heaton Road with its remnants being viewable only from them.

17

From the Wincheap Road to the south eastern outskirts of the city little remains of the railway. However, one curiosity leaps out at the explorer. Along Stuppington Lane, a country turning off South Canterbury Road, a bridge traverses the line. On one side, the cutting appears to have been filled in to the level of the bridge arch, presumably to provide the farmer with additional land for cultivation. Interestingly, the warehouse roofs of the Wincheap Industrial Estate are visible once again from this opposite direction.

On the other side of the bridge, looking toward the hospital and the long lost site of South Canterbury Station, the cutting has been part filled in to the rear of houses on South Canterbury Road   leaving just a small pit immediately by the bridge. Although the station was opened as South Canterbury, it later became   Canterbury South so that all the Canterbury stations had suffixes rather than   prefixes. Remarkably, only the South station was geographically correct.

In common with many remnant structures along the route of the line, the Bridge bears a painted inscription recording its cataloguing by BRB (Residuary) Ltd who are responsible for maintenance of structures on closed lines. Some, appear recently repainted, thereby, preserving the line's heritage. However, the inevitable, and shameful, graffiti accompanies it.

The South Canterbury Station has given way to staff residences for the Kent & Canterbury Hospital. All that remains is this bridge abutment on one side of the Nackington Road, heavily overgrown. More housing obscures the trackbed as the route of the line wends its way out of the city limits and on toward the village of Bridge. It is amusing, perhaps, to ponder on how useful the South Canterbury Station may have been today in serving the hospital and the Kent County Cricket Ground. The hospital layout would have had to have been different! This may not be an entirely fanciful notion. My photographer and friend, Andrew Garland, recalls a manager of his (a long time ago, of course) recounting how he used the line and how it was only ever busy when the cricket was on!

18

From South Canterbury To Bridge

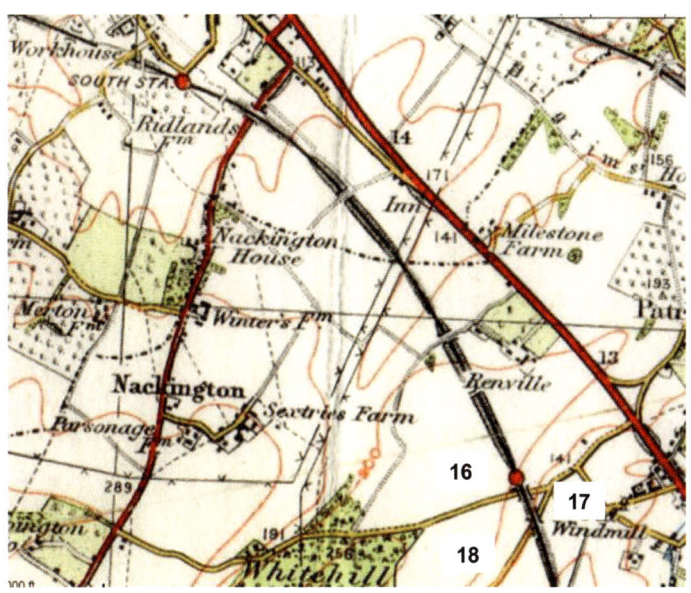

Reproduced from out of copyright OS Map 117 East Kent published 1938.

Leaving Nackington Road behind the route of the Elham Valley Railway can be traced from the air but little remains as it makes the relatively short distance to Bridge. In common with many lines in rural areas the railway station that served Bridge was some distance from the village. The station site is now part of a private residence but close by the abutments of the bridge that carried the railway over Bridge Road / Station Road can be seen. Almost immediately after, following the fork in the road toward Pett Bottom, the bridge that carried the line over Pett Bottom Road remains completely intact.

Below, this bridge is on the right in juxtaposition with the previous bridge's abutments out of shot (follow the tree line!) The white building on the far left of shot carries a fair deal of station type fenestration, however, the platforms are at right angles to it. The original station building and platforms remain in situ but are now a private residence not available for public viewing. Pett Bottom, according to Ian Fleming, is where James Bond lived with his aunt after his parents died.

From
Bridge
To
Bishopsbourne

Reproduced from out of copyright OS Map 117 East Kent published 1938.

Leaving Bridge Station behind, the remains of the route snake past the village itself until the Bourne Park estate is reached. By way of the footpath it is possible to appreciate the quirkiness of lines constructed at the time that placed village stations apart from the villages they served. In this photograph the footpath goes over the line
by the customary solid bridge and the church spire of the village church is a mere pin-prick someway in the distance.

The Bourne Park Estate is the location of the first of two tunnels on the line. Bourne Tunnel, whilst not absolutely necessary in an engineering sense, was constructed, it is recorded, so that the line would not spoil the magnificent views from the main residence of the estate. An earlier example of 'cut and cover' techniques later used to mitigate the effects of the High Speed link through Kent. Of course, the Bourne Park Estate is in private ownership, so access to the tunnel is not available without permission. (The author is grateful to the BRBR for permitting access.) The tunnel itself is 330 yards long and is the longest of the two tunnels on the Elham Valley Railway. The other is at Etchinghill and this tunnel features later.

A short distance further down the line the railway reaches the tiny village of Bishopsbourne. I am deeply indebted and grateful to the current owner of the former Bishopsbourne Railway Station who granted access to both this book's photographer and author. We spent a delightful few hours taking in this nostalgic and beautiful location. How wonderful it must be to live here!

It clearly is, judging by the enthusiasm of the owner for both his home and the restoration and preservation of this important piece of railway history. Readers should note that this is a private residence and respect the owner's privacy.

These splendid beer mats, commissioned by the station owner, are delightful. It is a wonder that guests would actually want to use them for their intended purpose!

Bishopsbourne Station, restored as a private residence, nestles happily amongst the trees, and can be seen from the bridge that carries Crows Camp Road across the former trackbed before it meanders south-east. The underneath of the bridge itself has been filled in to prevent collapse, no doubt.

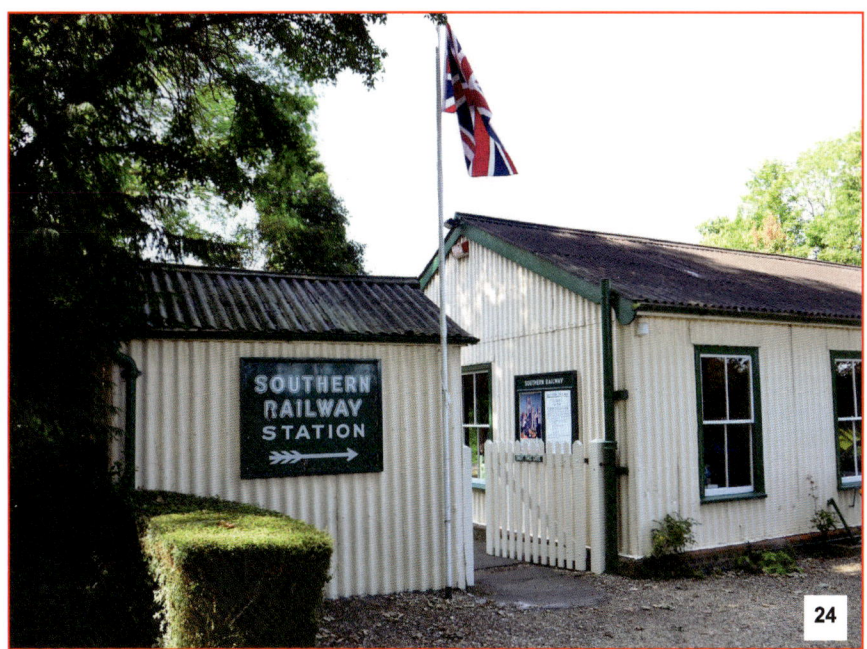

On down the station drive, the side gate leading to the down platform is reached. It is on this platform that the main station building, now a beautiful home, is located. The author is captured (below) gaining access. The Photographer is reflected, eerily, in the window of the building to the right of shot!

25

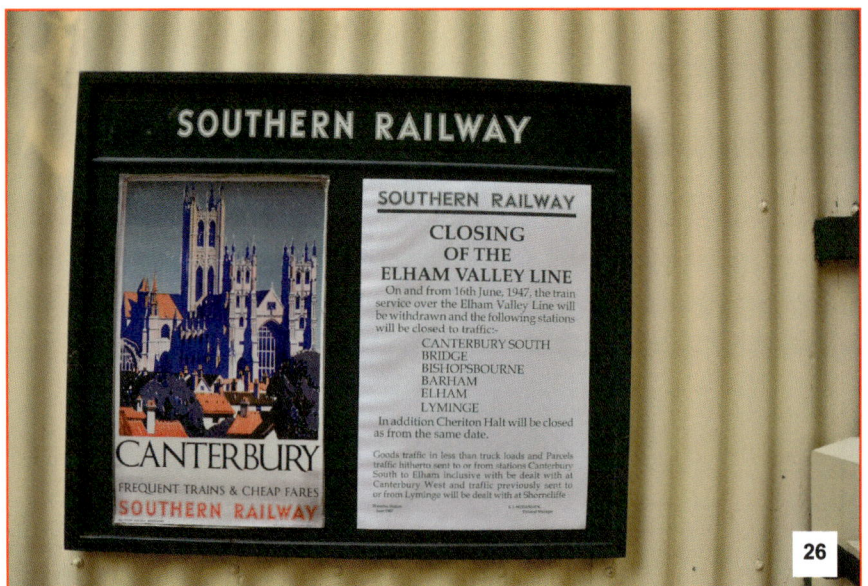

Entering the platform area, one is greeted with posters exalting the benefits of a day trip to Canterbury and notifying the impending closure of the line.

Present day use of the building (washing line!) sits harmoniously with the past.

28

On to the down platform and the years simply fall away. The luggage cart makes a handy log store for these buildings were never highly insulated and heating in winter is most certainly needed. It would not be hard to imagine this station receiving a 'best kept' award today.

Tastefully displayed are these replica notice-boards advertising the benefits of travelling by train and the destinations to which the traveller might be whisked away. Reminders all, of a long gone era, when even the smallest of stations had a part to play on the wider network.

29

30

27

Above: Looking north toward Canterbury.

Below: Looking south toward Folkestone.

Let us not forget, also, that goods and luggage may be weighed for safe loading in the baggage compartment or goods / brake van. The former door to the main internal structure now leads to a wonderful home lounge, itself adorned with memorabilia of the line's heyday.

The up platform has not been forgotten either, with benches restored or replicated.

The former booking clerk's office along with the station master's and porter's office have been converted to a kitchen but preserving as much of the railway style of the time as possible. The hatch through which tickets were purchased has been retained as a very handy serving hatch from the kitchen to the former main hall, now lounge.

And who would not have been pleased to have passed the time in the station buffet? This was, of course, not present in the original building as it occupies the space formerly used by the aforementioned staff offices. However, it is an extremely nice touch and, no doubt, is often used and much appreciated. Notice too, the photograph in the right hand corner. This is a print of that taken on the day that the then Prime Minister, Winston Churchill, visited Bishopsbourne Station to inspect the garrison that operated the 'Boche Buster.' The big field gun had been hauled to the platform from its stabling point for that purpose.

The double door to the down platform from the main station hall now leads directly from the living room but proudly displays, nevertheless, signs encouraging guests to show their tickets on their way 'To The Trains.'

The hard work of the current owner to restore Bishopsbourne Station and the loving way in which it now both encompasses the past and incorporates the present is little short of a masterpiece of montage.

I felt it a real wrench to leave the platform although it seems some may not as the starter semaphore signal indicates that there is a down train due bound for Folkestone!

The bridge immediately to the south of the station platforms has been filled in underneath and drainage provided. This and the parapet can be seen here also.

At the very least, however, I still have my platform ticket as a memento of my visit. Don't tell anyone my stay exceeded one hour though!

31

From Bishopsbourne To Barham

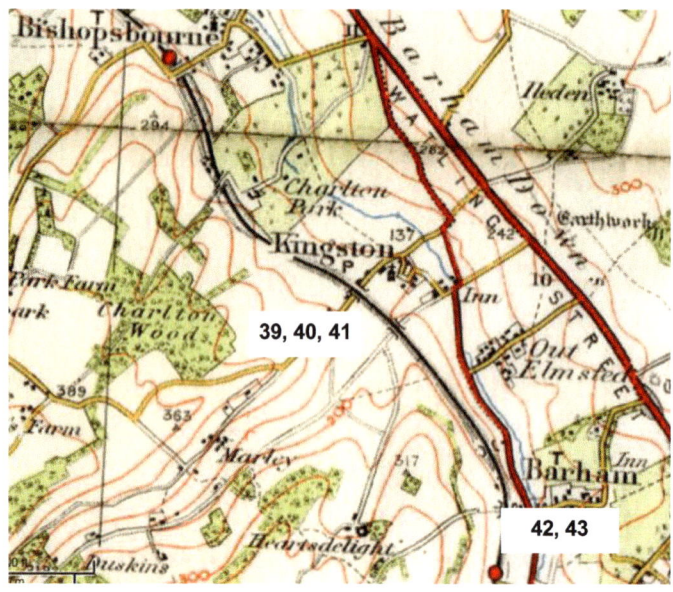

Reproduced from out of copyright OS Map 117 East Kent published 1938.

Approaching Kingston, more housing has engulfed the line but a short walk from the Black Robin Public House down Covet Lane reveals the bridge that took the line onward toward Barham. Once again the bridge is complete rather than having been reduced to just abutments.

From here the line makes its way toward Barham, where much of its route has been lost. The footpath runs alongside the line of trees marking the railway route itself. The embankment at Covet Lane is actually quite substantial and another example of the additional engineering challenges faced on the Lyminge to Canterbury section.

And here is a familiar sight on most abandoned railways.

Almost quintessentially English, rusted iron field gates amongst overgrown footpaths and disused railway trackbeds.

Almost comforting and reassuring!

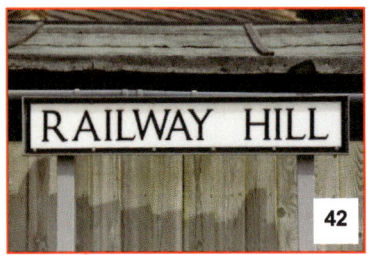

So, to the village of Barham. Here the railway station was sited relatively centrally, although now nothing remains.

A small clue perhaps in this street sign but the station site itself is completely overtaken by residential development.

All that remains here is on one side of the road, half of the bridge abutment carrying the line over Railway Hill whilst on the other side of the road, directly opposite, all trace has been lost.

On a happier note, maybe, the former Barham signal box can be viewed at the East Kent Light Railway headquarters at Shepherdswell.

From Barham To Elham

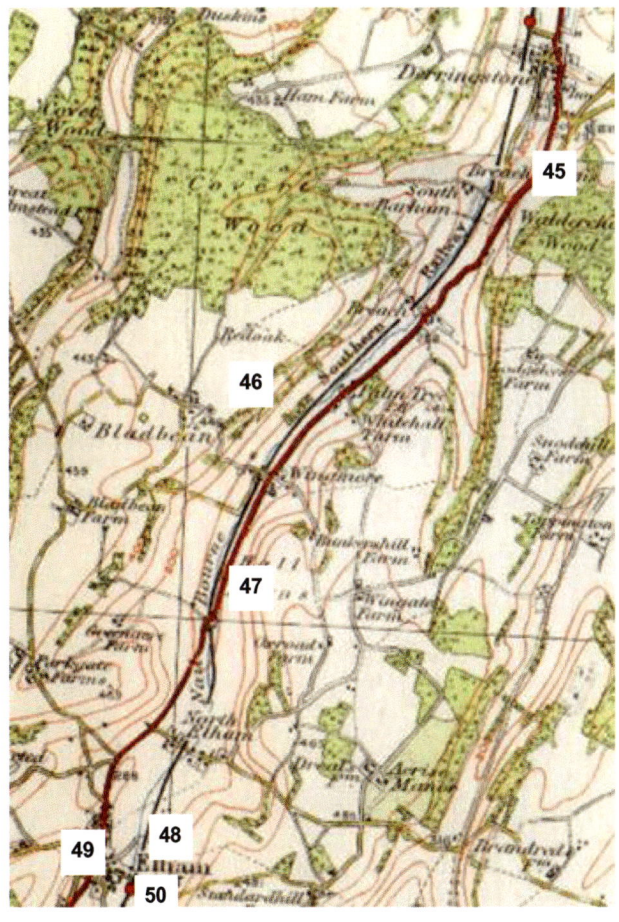

Reproduced from out of copyright OS Map 117 East Kent published 1938.

Much of the route on leaving Barham has disappeared over time since the closure of the line although a keen eye may discern its remnants to the right of the road travelling toward Elham, mostly following the route of the Nailbourne stream.

What delight if the idle walker could view a locomotive in full steam here with, perhaps, one of those new-fangled' bi-planes on right turnout from the nearby Clipgate airfield passing overhead!

Indeed, one bridge survives at the hamlet of Wingmore and carries the narrow road to Bladbean over the route.

Just past Wingmore, the route traverses the road to Elham. Originally, the road went over the railway by means of a dog-legged bridge known locally as 'the World's Wonder Bridge.' This substantial structure was, with difficulty, demolished in 1958. During the demolition, traffic had to come down onto the trackbed to make progress in either direction. Of course, the volume of road traffic was minimal compared to today. A photograph of the road engine needed to assist in the demolition is on display at the Peene Railway Museum.

Although the location is still in evidence nothing of the bridge remains. The road has long ago been brought down to the level of the trackbed and the dogleg is now a relatively fast straight.

At Elham, although the route may be discerned, the station itself has given way to a housing development. Some of the trackbed has been taken into the Elham Valley Way, a joy for walkers and horse riders alike, and where the Elham Valley Way deviates from the railway route, the course of the line may still be viewed. Here, the old trackbed makes its way toward the former Elham Station site. Note the Elham Valley Way marker.

And then across the road where the trackbed has been thoughtfully laid to lawn. An odd piece of land that it should be fenced in such a manner! It is part of the trackbed between the platforms and at this point a huge iron girder footbridge spanned the line so that passengers may gain access to, and egress from, the down platform. Very imposing for a country station!

Where once the station was, another housing estate has sprung up. This one, apparently, quite soon after the line closed.

The road, mentioned previously, can be seen snaking up the hill. (toward bottom right of picture.) The station itself would have been to the left of this road. The row of houses to the middle right marks the route of the line from the Canterbury direction and pre-dates the closure of the railway.

37

From Elham To Lyminge

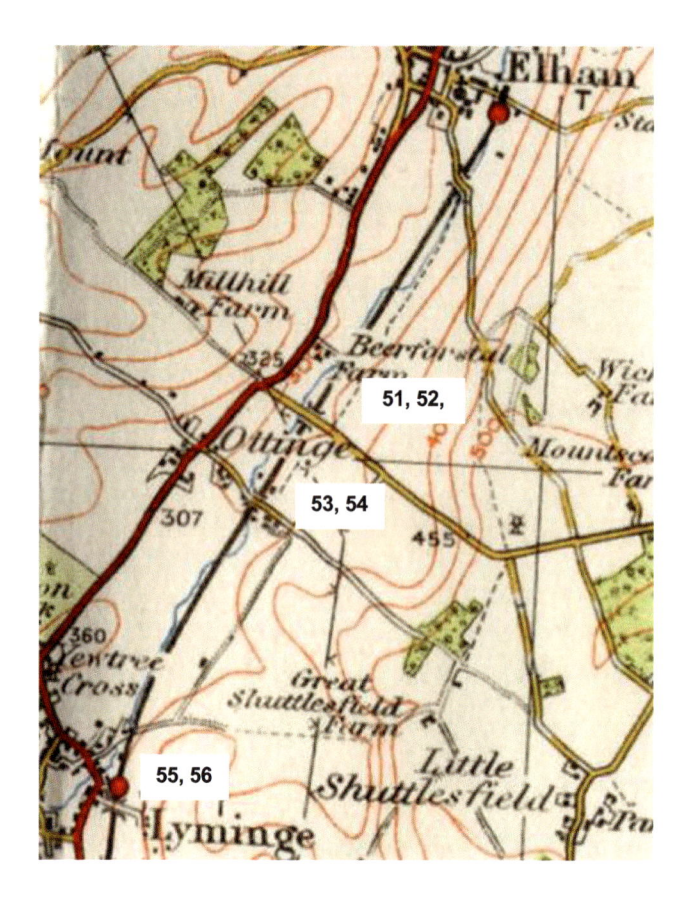

Reproduced from out of copyright OS Map 117 East Kent published 1938.

Leaving Elham behind, the railway route continues on to Lyminge arguably the home of the best preserved remnant apart from Bishopsbourne Station. Of course, that is in private ownership, whereas the old Lyminge Station is in Public ownership.

51

However, before that point is reached, two completely intact bridges carrying the road over the line may be observed. Both are at Ottinge, and in keeping with the high specification of engineering of the line, remain imposing. The first, numbered 2081, displays the now familiar major wing walls, almost, as if the bridge was a tunnel portal.

52

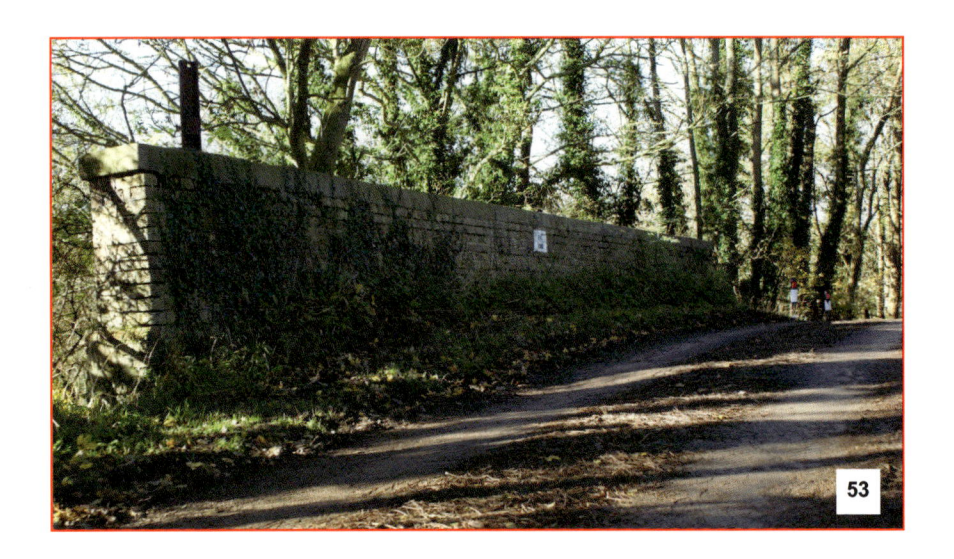

The second Ottinge bridge is no less imposing although the immediate trackbed on either side has been subsumed into the neighbouring residences' gardens.

55

And so to Lyminge where the station building is now a public library although the exterior retains its rural railway aesthetic. Regrettably, since the author last had the opportunity to visit this site some 25 years ago (circa 1977,) the then intact platforms have given way to a car park for new cottages built on the trackbed at the southern end. Part of the up platform is still visible but the down platform has completely disappeared. The up platform's barrelled canopy, which would have doubled the width of the building, had been removed some time ago, of course! It would seem that the station now sits in imperfect isolation to its modern surroundings where once it stood proud and dominant.

56

From Lyminge To Folkestone West

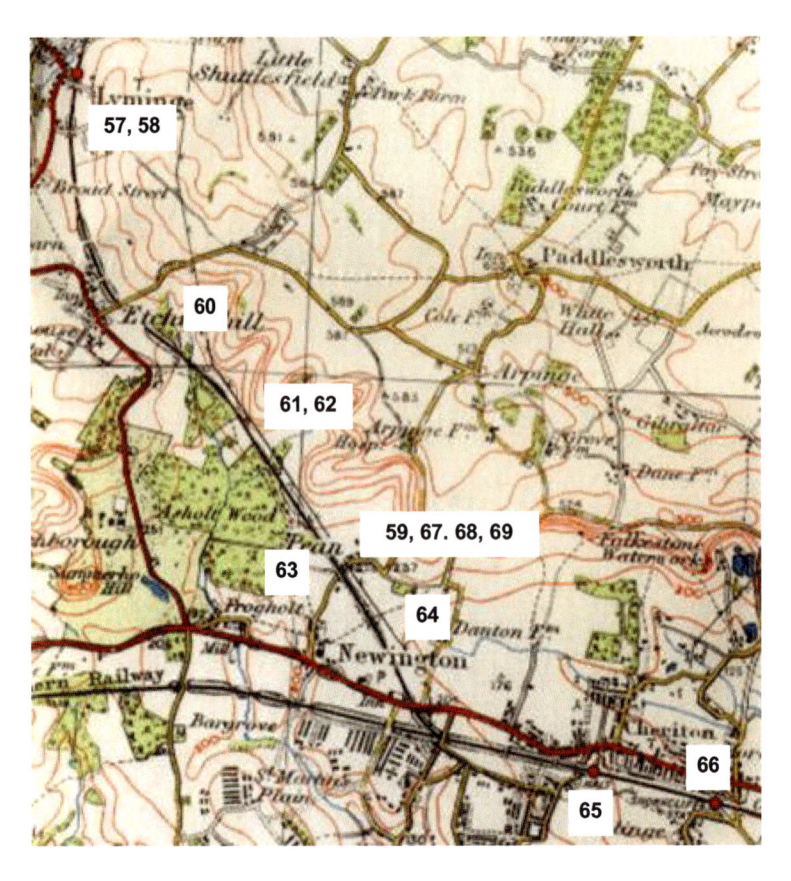

Reproduced from out of copyright OS Map 117 East Kent published 1938.

Lyminge station northern end trackbed has also been obliterated by housing development and each is characteristically termed "railway cottages" and "the Sidings" in deference to the past.

The 'railway cottages' stand between the station building and the adjacent Nash Hill bridge, blotting out the view of the station that existed in the late 1970s from the bridge , Progress!

57

A second Lyminge bridge may be viewed a short distance further on toward Etchinghill.

Greenbanks bridge, numbered 2088, again has tunnel type buttressing.

Regrettably, the trackbed at this point seems to have become a popular dumping ground.

58

From Lyminge to Etchinghill much of the line has been lost and what remains is not easily accessible. However, for the adventurous explorer there is reward to be had in exchange for a 45 minute hike along the trackbed, forming part of the Elham Valley Way, coming back toward Canterbury from Peene.

59

Just opposite the excellent Peene Railway Museum, the trackbed may be accessed up an incline. On a warm, but not too hot, sunny East Kent day, a pleasurable walk may be taken along the former trackbed. There is a cautionary note for walkers though. Signposts along the way remind the adventurer that a troop training area is being traversed! There is evidence of heavy military vehicles being driven along the softer parts of the old railway. Softer, because the hard surface gives way to more natural earth underfoot after the large embankment has given way to flat landscape and then to a deep cutting. In the cutting, trees have been permitted to slide down the bank, fall over in bad weather no doubt, with the result that the trackbed, although not impassable, can be difficult to navigate in places.

However, the reward, once tree trunks have been hurdled and undergrowth brushed aside, is worth it.

And this is the sight that will greet the adventurer; the southern portal to Etchinghill Tunnel.

The Etchinghill Tunnel is 97 yards long and remarkably well preserved. The northern portal, although showing light at the end of the tunnel, is inaccessible from the Etchinghill village end, again it is entered from a deep cutting now fully overgrown.

There are a number of interesting sights to take in along the walk to the southern portal. There are a couple of bridges that carry the railway over farm tracks linking fields either side of the high embankment. These are substantial bores through the embankment although the metal railings protecting any line-side walker from the drop below are now heavily rusted and, in places, removed from their former anchorages. There are also numerous inspection hatches and pits for the line drainage, encrusted with moss and lichen, of course.

It is recommended that this walk be conducted in summer, though, as clearly the drainage along this section of the line no longer functions and between October and April the ground underfoot can be decidedly "sloppy!"

Rusted railings atop a bridge providing farm access through the embankment.

Line-side drainage inspection pit in the cutting leading to the southern portal of Etchinghill tunnel.

Back at the Peene road, the Elham Valley Way veers away from the embankment down to the road then continues on the other side of the road toward Cheriton on account of the substantial span of the bridge carrying the line across the Peene road having been removed.

63

Unfortunately, after just a few hundred yards, although the top of the embankment may be regained, further progress on the former trackbed is halted by undergrowth, and the standard 'keep out' fencing.

In fact, from here on the route of the EVR is lost firstly to the Channel Tunnel Rail Terminal and then to the M20 motorway and development toward Cheriton and Folkestone.

47

![64]

In this photograph can be seen a Eurostar on Hi-Speed 1 (HS1,) a freight shuttle loading in the terminal, and a car shuttle on the loop from the tunnel to the terminal to unload. The car shuttle from the continent is visible behind and to the left of the Eurostar.

The loop runs under the terminal buildings, that occupy what would have been the track bed of the Elham Valley Railway so at least part of the old track bed is still actually seeing trains running!

The junction adjacent to Horn Street, Cheriton, has completely disappeared and the cutting infilled. The route at this point is only discernible by the curved nature of the rear gardens of the adjacent houses.

The site of Cheriton Halt (only ever used by Elham Valley Railway trains) is adjacent to the Risborough Lane bridge. The Halt itself was little more than a wooden structure and sat atop the embankment.

Trains do still run over the tracks, of course, as it is the mainline from Ashford to Dover via Folkestone.

![65]

66

Journey's end is at Folkestone West, originally styled Shorncliffe in Elham Valley Railway days.

Note here, that part of the down forecourt has been laid out to (road) coaches only bays. These are for the VSOE (Venice Simplon Orient Express) tours that transfer passengers from the Pullman train here for a few hours enjoying the sights of Folkestone before re-alighting for the trip back, normally, to London Victoria.

The Peene Railway Museum, run by the Elham Valley Line Trust, is dedicated to remembering the Elham Valley Railway and preserving such artefacts that may be obtained. The Trust and the Museum were founded by George Wright in the 1980s.

67

It also boasts a Countryside Centre housed in a 290 year old barn, carefully relocated from land now occupied by the Channel Tunnel Rail Terminal and painstakingly restored to house tea rooms, craft and display areas. It is known as George's Barn in honour of the Trust's founder.

68

69

50

70

71

The museum itself houses much memorabilia. Former station name signs from the Elham Valley Line are held ready to undergo restoration and, eventually, display. A third sign from Lyminge Station is held but this will take a considerable amount of restoration and re-fabrication as it survives in part only.

Of interest, are the 'n' gauge' models of the Elham Valley Line itself and the Channel Tunnel Rail Terminal. Many aspects along the line are represented on the working layout of the Elham Valley Line housed in a glass fronted case along one wall of the museum building. Those pictured here are a selection. Each scene is representative of how various elements would have looked. Of particular note are the faithfully recreated barrelled roofed platforms canopies

72

73

Lyminge Station

Elham Station

In the re-creation of Elham Station note the substantial footbridge. It is perhaps easier to see in this model, as the original no longer exists, the curiosity of the footbridge, given it's proximity to a level crossing so often used to cross the line by passengers at rural stations elsewhere in the land. In the model of the 'World's Wonder' Bridge at Wingmore / Bladbean, its dogged leg nature can be clearly seen.

The road has been straightened and is at track level (in the real world!). The model was designed and constructed by village models (www.villagemodels.co.uk) with the help of the Folkestone Model Railway Club.

74

51

The Channel Tunnel layout has its own building with viewing gallery. The layout itself was constructed in six months for the Channel Tunnel Rail Link share launch in London then moved to the Visitor Centre in Cheriton before being relocated to the Peene Railway Museum when the former closed. It represents the terminal on the English side of the English Channel. A second model of the French terminal was made and it had been hoped that this might be housed in an adjacent building (currently used as a workshop.) However, the model of the French Terminal has been lost and a new one would have to be created if this project were to be concluded. Rather cleverly the two buildings (if it comes to fruition) would be linked by 'The Channel Tunnel" into which a Shuttle is just about to dive in the picture above right.

The model is superby crafted and includes all the activity at the terminal. The main terminal building stands ready to receive passengers disembarking from coaches waiting for their turn to be loaded onto the trains. Lorries that might otherwise have gone by sea ferry traverse the roadways leading to the loading bays for the long trains of caged rolling stock.

52

Bibliography

The Elham Valley Railway by Michael Forwood
Phillimore 1975, ISBN 0 85033 110 2

The Elham Valley Line 1887-1947 by Brian Hart,
Wild Swan Publications 1984, ISBN: 0 906867 22 3.

Along the Elham Valley by Brian Hart,
Extract from the Railway Magazine March 1979

Branch Lines Around Canterbury by Vic Mitchell & Kevin Smith,
Middleton Press 1995, ISBN: 1 873793 58 8

The Elham Valley Line by A Earle Edwards,
Extract from the Southern Railway Magazine, August 1947

Acknowledgements

Special thanks go to the following without whom this book could not have been completed.

Jan Knott	owner of the former Bishopsbourne Railway Station (for your kindness in showing us your wonderful home)
Jackie Archer	Landlady, Mermaid Inn, Bishopsbourne (this pub is well worth a visit)
Gary Bullett	Peene Railway Museum (for all your help)
The Elham Valley Line Trust	(for your help in producing this book and for your dedication to preserving the memory of the line itself.)
Ordnance Survey Mapping	(for the use of old out of copyright maps that made sense of it all)
British Railways Board (Residuary) Ltd	(for granting permission to access structures)

Thanks also to the following who contributed, encouraged, advised, made helpful suggestions, gave tips, read and re-read drafts etc, etc. etc.

Sarah Ansell (www.sarahcanterbury.com)
Rebecca Arnold
Sheree Hyder
Ken Bradshaw
Ian Leach
Tony Millard
Bob Murchison
Phil Nicholson
Andrew Rowbottom (www.ponies.me.uk)
John Pullinger

and probably many, many others!

Additional photography:

Charlotte Guise

About the Photographer

Andrew Garland was also born in East Kent in 1955. School days in Faversham required a commute by train so his interest in Railways was born. Membership of the schools Railway Society soon followed, and unable to secure any of the official (important!) posts, he became the society photographer, a courtesy title held at the time because he was the only one with a camera!!.. albeit a box brownie!! A Civil Service career of 36 years followed and it was not until after this that Andrew finally acquired his first serious camera and set about combining a passing interest in photography with his lifelong passion for the railway. Married with two grown up children, Andrew's other interests of cycling and gardening keep him fit and busy. A bit of a dinosaur himself, and like most others, Andrew does not use social media...yet.

Despite being born in the same year, living in the same area, and having several shared interests, including railways and following the same football team, it was not until the mid 1970's when another mutual interest, in community radio, finally brought Peter & Andrew together.

Comments on this title and any suggestions for future titles may be sent by email to:

railwayremnants@gmail.com

Published by:

Peter Guise

railwayremnants@gmail.com

Content copyright © Peter Guise 2013

Photography copyright © Andrew Garland 2013 & © Peter Guise 2013

All rights reserved. No portion of this book may be reproduced, stored in a retrieval system or transmitted at any time or by any means mechanical, electronic, photocopying, recording or otherwise without the prior written permission of the publisher.

The right of Peter Guise to be identified as the author of this work has been asserted by him in accordance with the Copyright, Designs and Patents Act 1988.

First printed November 2012

Made in Charleston, South Carolina, USA by createspace

ISBN 9781481002882

CPSIA information can be obtained
at www.ICGtesting.com
Printed in the USA
LVIC06n1439031215
465226LV00002B/24